# Make Your Own
# Purses
## & Bags

# Anna-Marie D'Cruz

**PowerKiDS**
press

New York

Published in 2009 by The Rosen Publishing Group Inc.
29 East 21st Street, New York, NY 10010

First Edition

Senior Editor: Jennifer Schofield
Designer: Jason Billin
Project maker: Anna-Marie D'Cruz
Photographer: Chris Fairclough
Proofreader: Susie Brooks

Library of Congress Cataloging-in-Publication Data

D'Cruz, Anna-Marie.
   Make your own purses and bags / Anna-Marie D'Cruz. — 1st ed.
      p. cm. — (Do it yourself projects!)
   Includes index.
   ISBN 978-1-4358-2856-8 (library binding)
   ISBN 978-1-4358-2929-9 (paperback)
   ISBN 978-1-4358-2930-5 (6-pack)
   1. Handbags—Juvenile literature. 2. Recycling (Waste, etc.)—
Juvenile literature. I. Title.
   TT667.D37 2009
   646.4'8—dc22

                                            2008033671

Manufactured in China

Acknowledgments
All photography Chris Fairclough except:
page 4 right: Werner Foreman/CORBIS; page 4 left:
Richard Cummins/CORBIS; page 5: right: Rob Howard/
CORBIS; page 7 bottom right: Catherine Carnow/CORBIS

### Note to parents and teachers:
The projects in this book are designed
to be made by children. However, we
do recommend adult supervision at all
times since the Publisher cannot be held
responsible for any injury caused while
making the projects.

# Contents

# All about bags & purses

We use bags and purses every day for carrying and storing things and keeping things safe. Bags and purses come in many shapes and sizes, from small wallets to bigger gym bags.

## PURSES FROM LONG AGO

People have used bags and purses throughout history. The Ancient Romans used a drawstring leather pouch that was hung from a belt to hold their heavy coins. The Ancient Egyptians made baskets and bags from materials such as reeds and grasses. The Native Americans made a pouch, known as a parfleche, from buffalo hide (see right) to keep their belongings safe.

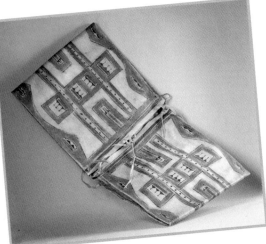

For some time, pouches were worn on the outside of clothes, tied on around the waist, such as a Scottish sporran (see left). A sporran is a pouch attached to a belt and worn over a kilt. Pouches on the outside were often snatched so people began to wear them under their clothes. Today, it is not just money that people keep safe in bags—cellphones, walkmans, and MP3 players are all carried in purses, bags, and cases of different shapes and sizes.

# DIFFERENT MATERIALS

Modern purses and bags are made from a variety of materials, depending on their use. Some bags, such as rucksacks (see right) and briefcases, are waterproof. This means that the things inside them will stay dry on a rainy day. Handbags and wallets are often made from leather so that they last a long time. The leather can also be dyed, so the bags and wallets come in lots of different colors. Other bags, such as grocery bags, are made from paper and plastic. Plastic bags are not only strong so that you can put lots of things in them, but often they can be recycled, so they are good for the environment, too.

# GET STARTED!

This book shows you how to make different bags and purses. When you make your projects, try to use materials that you already have, either at home or at school. For example, for card, use the back of used notepads, art pads, and empty cereal boxes. For the fabric in these projects, old, but clean clothes, pillowcases, bedsheets, and towels are ideal. Reusing and recycling materials like this is good for the environment and will save you money. The projects have all been made and decorated for this book, but do not worry if yours look a little different—just have fun making and using your bags and purses.

# Didgeridoo pencil case

The didgeridoo is a musical instrument used by the Aboriginal people of Australia. Didgeridoos are made from the branches of eucalyptus trees that have been hollowed out by termites. Follow the steps to make your own didgeridoo-style pencil case.

## YOU WILL NEED

colored paper

empty potato chip tube with lid

pair of scissors

pencil

extra paper

newspaper

paints

paintbrush

double-sided tape

**1** Cut a sheet of colored paper large enough to wrap around the tube.

**2** Think about the patterns and pictures you want as part of your design. Do some rough drawings on some spare paper.

**3** When you are happy with your design, draw it on the colored paper cut in Step 1.

**4** Cover your work surface with newspaper. Paint the design with bright-colored paint and allow it to dry. To make the pattern look more Aboriginal, dab on dots of paint and use crosshatching to shade it.

**5** When the paint is dry, use double-sided tape to attach the paper to the tube. Your didgeridoo pencil case is ready to try out.

## ABORIGINAL ART

Often, didgeridoos are decorated by burning or painting the wood. The patterns, dots, symbols, and other designs have particular meaning to the Aborigine who decorated them.

# Mini parfleche

The parfleche is a large, flat, rectangular bag used by Native Americans to carry food and clothing. The bags were traditionally made from buffalo hide and they were hung from the saddles of horses. Make your own miniature parfleche to keep your things safe.

## YOU WILL NEED

- light-colored large card
- black felt-tip pen
- ruler
- pair of scissors
- hole punch
- pencil
- colored pencils
- string or shoelace

**1** Place the card with shortest sides at the top and bottom. Using a black felt-tip pen and ruler, draw a line across the card that is that is 4¼ in. (11cm) from the top of the card and a line that is 4¼ in. (11cm) from the bottom of the card. Then draw a line 3 in. (8cm) in from the right-hand side and another line 3 in. (8cm) in from the left-hand side of the card.

**2** Draw lines across the corners of the card where the lines meet the edge of the card. Cut across these lines so that you have an octagon (eight-sided shape).

**3** Use a hole punch to make holes where shown.

8

**4** Turn the card over so that the lines are face down. Use a pencil to draw a geometric pattern on the longer inner section of the card. Go over the design with a black felt-tip pen and color it in with colored pencils.

**5** Turn the card over so that the pattern is facing down. Fold the longer sides in along the lines drawn in Step 1. Put the things you are keeping in the parfleche underneath the flaps. Thread some string through the holes and tie the sides together.

**6** Fold over the short ends along the lines drawn in Step 1. Tie these ends together to keep your belongings safe.

## NATIVE AMERICANS

Native Americans are the original inhabitants of North America. Traditionally, they hunted animals such as buffalo, which roamed the plains. The animals were killed for food and they also provided Native American people with hides to make clothing and tepees.

# Funky wallet

A wallet is a pocket-sized bag. Usually, wallets have different sections for holding paper money, cards, and coins. Reuse an old plastic tablecloth to make your own new wallet.

**1** Use a pencil and ruler to draw the following shapes on the tablecloth: two rectangles 10 x 4¾ in. (25 x 12cm), one rectangle 2¾ x 11 in. (7 x 28cm), and two squares 3¼ x 3¼ in. (8 x 8cm). Cut out all the shapes.

**2** Using the picture as a guide, stick tape along the edges, covering the patterned side by about ⅝ in. (1.5cm).

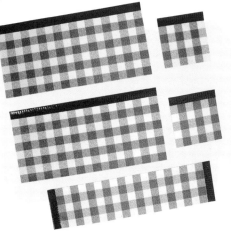

**3** To make a coin pouch, place the 2¾ x 11 in. (7 x 28cm) rectangle pattern-side down, with the short edge at the top and bottom. Fold up the rectangle from the bottom by 4¼ in. (11cm).

**4** Place one of the 10 x 4¾ in. (25 x 12cm) rectangles pattern-side up and with the taped edge away from you. Put the coin pouch in the middle of the rectangle and tape it along the sides.

**5** Place one of the square pieces of tablecloth pattern-side up on the left-hand side of the coin pouch. Line up the pieces at the bottom. Tape down the square along the right-hand side, overlapping the square piece by about ⅝ in. (1.5cm). Repeat this with the other square on the right-hand side, taping it down on the left-hand side.

**6** Lay the second 10 x 4¾ in. (25 x 12cm) rectangle pattern-side down and with the taped edge away from you. Place the rectangle from step 5 pattern-side up on top, and tape the two together along the sides and bottom edge, overlapping the pocketed side by about ⅝ in. (1.5cm).

**7** Use strong glue to stick one half of the velcro to the underside of the coin pouch flap. Glue the other half of the velcro to the middle of the coin pouch, so that when the flap is closed the two halves meet. Your wallet is now ready to use.

## FANTASTIC PLASTIC

Plastic is a tough, waterproof material. It is used to make all kinds of things, from toys and toothbrushes to telephones and bottles. Plastic was accidentally discovered by J. Paul Hogan and Robert L. Banks while they were trying to make fuel. During their experiments, they realized that their machines had become blocked with a sticky white substance. This white substance became known as plastic.

# MP3-player case

This pocket-sized case is similar to the Celtic bags worn by men, called sporrans. But this bag is not going on a belt. Instead, it is small enough to fit snugly in your pocket.

**1** Cut a piece of felt that will wrap around your MP3 player one and a half times and is 1½ in. (4cm) wider than the player.

**2** Use the pair of scissors to round off one end of the felt. This will become the flap end of the bag.

**3** Place the felt with the rounded end away from you, and place your MP3 player in the middle. Fold the felt up from the bottom so that it covers the MP3 player.

**4** Mark where you would like the button to be with a pencil or chalk. Sew the button in place (see page 13).

**5** Lay the fabric down in front of you with the button side down and the rounded end away from you. Fold it up from the bottom by enough to cover the MP3 player. Make a mark so you know how far up this is.

12

**6** Using a running stitch (see page 16), sew the two layers together along one side, up to the mark you made in in Step 5. Sew ½ in. (1cm) in from the edge. Turn back and repeat the running stitch through the stitches already sewn.

**7** Sew up the other side in the same way.

## SEWING ON BUTTONS

1. Thread a needle and knot one end.
2. Hold the button where you want it to be. Push the needle up from underneath the fabric and up through one hole of the button.
3. Take the needle down through the diagonally opposite hole and through the fabric.
4. Repeat this 3–4 times through the same holes.
5. Do the same through the other two holes.
6. Take the thread back through to underneath the fabric and knot it.

**8** Fold down the flap and feel where it covers the center of the button. Mark this with a pencil or chalk. Make a snip with the scissors that is long enough for the button to go through.

**9** Sew on a small piece of fun fur and add some tassels to decorate your bag. It is now ready to try out. You could make a case in the same way for a cellphone.

# Halloween bag

What we know as Halloween was originally part of the Celtic celebration of New Year, known as Samhain. Today on Halloween, people carve pumpkins and many children dress up in costumes, going from door to door trick-or-treating. Follow these simple steps to make your own pumpkin-shaped treat bag to hold all your goodies.

**1** From the long edge of the orange foam sheet, measure and cut out a strip that is 4 in. (10cm) wide and 16 in. (40cm) long. From the remaining foam, cut two circles that are about 8 in. (20cm) in diameter. You may find it helpful to draw around a plate for this.

**2** Place the edge of one circle against the edge of the strip of foam. Staple them together, about ½ in. (1cm) in from the edge. Continue stapling around the circle, keeping the edges together.

**3** Staple the second circle in the same way.

14

**4** Draw and cut out shapes at the opened end of both circles to make handles.

**5** To give your pumpkin bag a face, cut out eye, nose, and mouth shapes from the black foam sheet. Using double-sided tape, tape them to the bag. Your bag is ready to fill with delicious treats! You could change the color and decorations on this bag to make a bag for Easter or Christmas.

# Drawstring gym bag

Small drawstring bags were originally used for carrying coins. Gradually, the bags became bigger and in the eighteenth and nineteenth centuries, ladies carried their handkerchiefs in drawstring bags called reticules. Follow the steps to makes your own drawstring gym bag.

## YOU WILL NEED

fabric 14 x 36 in. (35 x 90cm)
thread
sewing needle
pair of scissors
72 in. (180cm) piping
safety pin

**1** Fold the fabric in half with the right sides facing each other.

## GET SEWING

To sew a running stitch, start by threading a needle. Tie a knot at one end of the thread. Push the point of the needle down through the fabric. Bring the needle back up again at a point farther forward from where you went down. Repeat this to give a row of stitches that look the same on both sides of the fabric.

**2** Knot one end of the thread, and thread the other end onto the needle. Sew a running stitch along one side of the fabric ¾ in. (2cm) in from the edge, starting at the folded edge. Stop stitching about 2¾ in. (7cm) from the top. Turn back and repeat the running stitch through the stitches already sewn. When you reach the end, knot the thread to keep it in place. Sew up the other side of the bag in the same way.

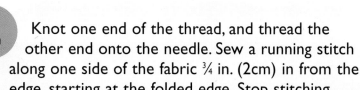

**3** Turn the bag inside out so that the fabric is the correct way around. Taking one side at a time, turn the top over to the inside by 1¼ in. (3cm) and sew a running stitch all along, ¾ in. (2cm) from the top. Turn back and repeat the running stitch through the stitches already sewn. This will make a tube for the piping to pass through.

**4** Snip a hole 2 in. (5cm) in from the bottom corner of one side of the bag. Thread one end of the piping through the hole, and knot it tightly around the corner.

**5** Attach a safety pin to the other end of the piping. Place it in the tube at the top of the bag on the same side as the knot. Wriggle the safety pin and piping along the tube around both sides of the bag.

**6** Bring the piping back out at the side where you started and take it back to the corner. Unhook the safety pin and thread the piping through the hole. Knot it tightly around the corner. Your bag is ready to try—put some gym shoes in the bag and sling it over your shoulder!

# Magic wallet

Keep your money and cards in this wallet. Be careful though, this wallet has magical properties, and you may find that your money is not where you left it!

## YOU WILL NEED

2 pieces of card, 3¼ x 4½ in. (8 x 11cm)

adhesive-backed plastic, fabric, or wrapping paper

glue (if using fabric or wrapping paper)

pair of scissors

ruler

piece of ¼ in. (5mm) wide elastic, 31½ in. (80cm) long

stapler

**1** Cover each side of both pieces of card with adhesive-backed plastic, fabric, or paper. When dry, lay the two rectangles next to each other.

**2** Staple one end of the elastic to the top left-hand edge of the left card, 1¼ in. (3cm) down from the top.

**3** Take the elastic under the left-hand card and over the top of the right-hand card. Staple it in place, slightly stretching the elastic.

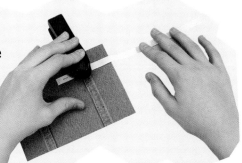

**4** Take the elastic diagonally across the back of the right-hand card and across the front of the left-hand card.

**5** Staple the elastic in place as shown.

**6** Take the elastic under the bottom of the left-hand card and over the top at the bottom of the right-hand card. Staple it in place.

**7** Take the elastic behind and diagonally across back of the card, and bring it back out at the top of card but below the earlier elastic. Staple it in place, but make sure you do not staple the elastic running behind the card. Cut off any spare elastic.

**8** Turn the wallet over and you should have one side with an "x" of elastic. On the other side, you should have two parallel lines.

**9** Try out the wallet by placing something under the "x" or the parallel lines, then flip the other side over and over again. The card magically moves under the parallel elastic!

# Magazine bag

Use an old pillowcase to make a bag for carrying some of your favorite magazines and comic books. You will need an adult to help you with some of the steps in this project.

## YOU WILL NEED

clean, old pillowcase
pair of scissors
pencil or piece of chalk
ruler
¾ in. (2cm) wide iron-on hemming tape
iron and ironing board

**1** Turn your pillowcase inside out. Use scissors to cut off the stitching from both sides of the pillowcase, keeping as close to the edge of the stitching as possible. Open out the pillowcase.

**2** Cut a 24 in. (60cm) width of fabric from one end of the opened pillowcase. This will make the main part of the bag. From the remaining fabric, cut two strips that are 4 in. (10cm) wide and as long as the fabric. These will make the two handles.

24 in. (60cm)

4 in. (10cm)

4 in. (10cm)

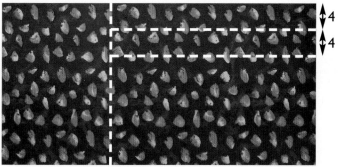

**3** Cut two pieces of iron-on hemming tape the same length as the handles. Place the handles in front of you with the wrong sides up. Put the hemming tape along the edge of each handle. Fold each handle in half along the length. Ask an adult to iron the fabric and hemming tape, following the instructions on the package.

**4** Cut two pieces of hemming tape the same length as the shortest side of the main part of the bag. Place the rectangle of fabric in front of you with the wrong side up and the shortest side at the top. Turn over the top edge by 1¼ in. (3cm). Place a strip of hemming tape underneath the fold.

**5** Place the ends of one of the straps on top of the hemming tape, making sure the strap is not twisted. Lay the second piece of hemming tape on top. Turn down the fold of fabric. Ask an adult to iron the fold in place.

**6** Ask an adult to help you iron the second strap to the other end of the rectangle in the same way.

**7** Bend the straps up and ask an adult to iron a double layer of hemming tape between the straps and the top of the bag to hold the straps in place.

**8** Fold the bag up with the right sides together. Place a double layer of hemming tape between the fabric along one side of the bag. Ask an adult to iron on the hemming tape. Repeat for the other side, and then turn the bag inside out.

# Glossary

**Aborigine**

A person who lived in Australia before the Europeans settled there. There are still Aboriginal people living in Australia today.

**Celtic**

Belonging to the people who lived in Britain before the Romans settled there.

**didgeridoo**

A musical instrument that is traditionally played by the Aborigines of Australia.

**eucalyptus tree**

A very tall evergreen tree found in Australia. The oil from the eucalyptus leaf is often used in medicines.

**experiment**

A scientific test that is done to see what happens.

**fuel**

Something that is burned to make heat or power, such as coal or oil.

**Halloween**

The festival that happens each year on October 31. Halloween was traditionally part of the Celtic New Year celebrations.

**hide**

The skin of an animal.

**kilt**

A kind of pleated skirt that is traditionally worn by Scottish men.

**material**

Anything used for making something else. Leather, metal, wood, and plastic are all materials.

**Native Americans**

The people who are native to North America and who lived there before European settlers arrived. Native Americans are divided into many different tribes, including the Cheyenne, Cherokee, Hopi, Tlingit, and Sioux.

**recycling**

To recycle something is to change it or treat it so that it can be used again. For example, the metal in soda cans can be recycled into other metal things.

**reusing**

To use something for a different purpose. For example, if you use the cardboard from a cereal box to make a project, you are reusing the cardboard.

### running stitch

A simple stitch where the thread is worked in and out of the fabric. The stitches can be short or long.

### sporran

A pouch that is worn by Scottish men at the front of their kilt. Sporrans are usually made of leather and covered in fur.

### termite

An insect that is known for eating through wood. Sometimes, termites are called white ants.

### trick-or-treating

When children knock on people's doors at Halloween, asking for treats. If people do not give children candy, the children may play a trick on them.

### uniform

The special clothes and shoes that a person uses to play sports. For example, a soccer uniform consists of a shirt, shorts, shoes, and shin pads.

### waterproof

Something that water cannot get into. Some materials, such as certain types of plastic, are waterproof.

# FURTHER INFORMATION

## BOOKS TO READ

**DIY Kids**
by Ellen Lupton and Julia Lupton
(Princeton Architectural Press, 2007)

**The Hip Handbag Book**
by Sherri Haab
(Watson Guptill, 2004)

## WEB SITES

Due to the changing nature of Internet links, PowerKids Press has developed an online list of Web sites related to the subject of this book. This site is updated regularly. Please use this link to access this list:
www.powerkidslinks.com/diyp/purses

# Index

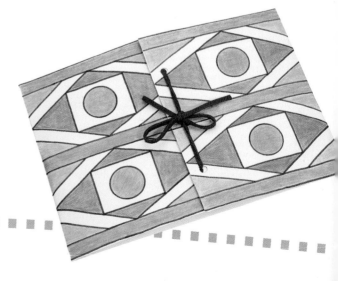